JEWELLERY FROM
CLASSICAL LANDS

REYNOLD HIGGINS

JEWELLERY
FROM
CLASSICAL
LANDS

PUBLISHED BY
THE TRUSTEES OF
THE BRITISH MUSEUM
1969

PRINTED IN GREAT BRITAIN
AT THE UNIVERSITY PRESS, OXFORD
BY VIVIAN RIDLER
PRINTER TO THE UNIVERSITY

CONTENTS

ACKNOWLEDGEMENTS

A number of the illustrations in this book have previously appeared in my book *Greek and Roman Jewellery*. I am grateful to the publishers, Methuen & Co. Ltd, for permission to reproduce them. I would also like to thank my wife for reading the text and making many helpful suggestions.

LIST OF PLATES

Simple numbers refer to the *Catalogue of Jewellery*. Numbers prefaced by the letter R refer to the *Catalogue of Finger Rings*. Numbers in the form 1960. 11–1. 1 are the registration numbers of uncatalogued objects. All objects are of gold or electrum unless otherwise stated.

COLOURED PLATES

A. Nos. 1128–30. Pectoral ornaments, from Camirus in Rhodes. Greek, seventh century B.C. Ht. 1¾ in.

B. (*Centre*) No. 1608. Centre-piece of a diadem, inlaid with garnet. Provenance unknown. Hellenistic, second century B.C. L. 3¼ in. (*Outside*) No. 1947. Necklace, from Melos. Hellenistic, third century B.C. L. 13¼ in.

C. No. 1376. Fibula, from Vulci. Etruscan, seventh century B.C. L. 7¼ in.

D. No. 2746. Necklace, set with sapphire, garnet, and crystal, from Rome. Roman, first century A.D. L. 12⅝ in.

BLACK AND WHITE PLATES

1. MINOAN JEWELLERY, SEVENTEENTH CENTURY B.C.

A. No. 761. Pendant, provenance unknown. L. 4¼ in.

B. No. 762. Pendant (nature-god), provenance unknown. Ht. 2½ in.

2. MINOAN AND MYCENAEAN JEWELLERY, SIXTEENTH TO THIRTEENTH CENTURIES B.C.

A. R 873. Finger-ring, from Ialysus in Rhodes. L. of bezel 1 in.

B. No. 623. Pomegranate pendant, from Enkomi in Cyprus (?). Ht. ⅞ in.

C. R 690. Finger-ring, inlaid with lapis lazuli, provenance unknown. L. of bezel ¾ in.

D. No. 803. Plaque, Minoan goddess, provenance unknown. Ht. ¾ in.

E. 72. 3–15. 13. Plaque, rosette, from Ialysus in Rhodes. Diam. 1¼ ins.

F. Nos. 793–4. Two double-argonaut beads, from Ialysus in Rhodes. L. ½ in.

G. 1960. 11–1. 1. Lily bead, from Athens (?). Ht. ⅜ in.

H. No. 538. Ear-ring, from Maroni in Cyprus. Ht. 1⅛ in.

I. 1959. 2–14. 2. Flower or shell bead, provenance unknown. Ht. ½ in.

J. No. 348. Ear-ring, from Enkomi in Cyprus. Diam. 1 in.

K. No. 299. Ear-ring, from Enkomi in Cyprus. Diam. ⅝ in.

3. GREEK JEWELLERY, ELEVENTH TO EIGHTH CENTURIES B.C.

A. 1960. 11–1. 46. Fibula, from Athens (?). Eighth century B.C. L. 2⅛ in.

B. 1960. 11–1. 36. Finger-ring, from Athens (?). Ninth century B.C. Diam. ⅞ in.

C. 1960. 11–1. 11. Hair-ring, from Athens (?). Eleventh century B.C.
Diam. ¾ in.

D. 1960. 11–1. 41. Finger-ring, from Athens (?). Ninth–eighth century B.C.
Diam. ⅞ in.

E. 1960. 11–1. 18. Ear-ring, from Athens (?). Eighth century B.C. Diam. of
stud, 1¼ in.

F. No. 1240. Ear-ring, from Athens. Eighth century B.C. Ht. 1⅞ in.

4. SEVENTH-CENTURY GREEK JEWELLERY

A. No. 1035. Brooch, from Ephesus. Diam. 1 in.

B. No. 959. Pin, from Ephesus. L. 2½ in.

C. No. 1037. Brooch, from Ephesus. Ht. 1¼ in.

D. No. 1230. Rosette from diadem, provenance unknown. Diam. 1¾ in.

E. No. 1108. Pectoral ornament, from Camirus in Rhodes. Ht. 1¼ in.

F. No. 1160. Diadem, from Camirus in Rhodes. L. 1 ft.

5. 1959. 7–20. 1. SILVER WREATH, PROVENANCE UNKNOWN.
GREEK, FIFTH CENTURY B.C. HT. 6¾ IN.

6. GREEK JEWELLERY, FIFTH AND FOURTH CENTURIES B.C.

A. No. 1585. Ear-ring, provenance unknown. Ht. 1⅜ in.

B. No. 1646. Ear-ring, from Amathus in Cyprus. Diam. 1⅛ in.

C. R. 218. Finger-ring, from Tarentum. L. of bezel ⅞ in.

D. No. 1653. Ear-ring, from Eretria. Ht. 2⅜ in.

E. R. 42. Finger-ring, from South Italy. Diam. of bezel 1 in.

F. 1963. 5–24. 1a. Rosette, provenance unknown. Diam. 1⅜ in.

G. No. 2067. Ear-ring, from Camirus in Rhodes. Diam. ⅞ in.

7. NO. 1952. NECKLACE, FROM TARENTUM. GREEK, EARLY
FOURTH CENTURY B.C. L. 12¼ IN.

8. GREEK BRACELETS, FIFTH AND FOURTH CENTURIES B.C.

A. No. 1985. From Curium in Cyprus. Diam. 3¼ in.

B. 1957. 8–9. 1. Graeco-Scythian, inlaid with glass, unknown provenance.
Diam. 3⅛ in.

9. TERRACOTTA D 786. ETRUSCAN PORTRAIT FIGURE FROM
A SARCOPHAGUS. FROM CHIUSI. ABOUT 150 B.C.

10. HELLENISTIC JEWELLERY, 330–27 B.C.

A. No. 2426. Ear-ring, threaded with agate, provenance unknown. L. 1¼ in.

B. No. 1804. Ear-ring, inlaid with garnet, provenance unknown. Diam. 1 in.

C. No. 2063. Brooch, provenance unknown. Diam. 1⅜ in.

D. No. 1889. Ear-ring, from Cyme in Asia Minor. Ht. 1¼ in.

E. No. 2335. Ear-ring, with garnet pendant, from Vulci. Ht. 1¼ in.

F. R 936. Finger-ring, provenance unknown. Diam. ¾ in.

G. R 714. Finger-ring, with garnet bezel, from Crete. L. of bezel 1¼ in.

11. HELLENISTIC JEWELLERY, 330–27 B.C.

A. No. 2113. Diadem, from Santa Eufemia in South Italy. Ht. 1⅜ in.

B. No. 1975. Necklace of gold, glass and garnet, provenance unknown. L. 16¼ in.

C. No. 1989. Bracelet, from Cyme in Asia Minor. Diam. 3⅛ in.

12. ETRUSCAN BRACELETS, SEVENTH CENTURY B.C.

A. No. 1358. From Tarquinii. L. 6½ in.

B. No. 1356. From Praeneste. L. 7¼ in.

13. ETRUSCAN JEWELLERY, SEVENTH AND SIXTH CENTURIES B.C.

A. No. 1310. Ear-ring, from Vulci. Diam. 1½ in.

B. No. 1294. Ear-ring, from Chiusi. Ht. ¾ in.

C. No. 1419. Ear-ring, inlaid with glass, provenance unknown. Diam. 1⅜ in.

D. No. 1453. Necklace of gold, glass, and faience, provenance unknown. L. 6⅞ in.

14. ETRUSCAN JEWELLERY, 400–250 B.C.

A. No. 2252. Ear-ring, from Populonia. Ht. 2⅜ in.

B. R 355. Finger-ring, from Tarquinii. L. of bezel 1½ in.

C. No. 2230. Ear-ring, from Populonia. Ht. 1⅝ in.

D. No. 2271. Necklace, from Tarquinii. L. 18¼ in.

15. ROMAN JEWELLERY, 27 B.C.–A.D. 337.

A. No. 2619. Ear-ring, from Pozzuoli. Ht. 1¼ in.

B. No. 2668. Ear-ring, set with garnets, provenance unknown. Ht. 2⅛ in.

C. No. 2623. Ear-ring, set with emeralds, provenance unknown. Ht. ¾ in.

D. No. 2856. Fibula, provenance unknown. L. 3 in.

E. R 792. Finger-ring, with emerald bezel, provenance unknown. Diam. ¾ in.

F. R 987. Finger-ring, provenance unknown. Diam. ¾ in.

G. 1924. 5–14. 3. Finger-ring with beryl bezel and niello inscription, from Beaurains in France. Diam. ⅞ in.

16. ROMAN JEWELLERY, 27 B.C.–A.D. 337.

A. 1946. 7–2. 1. Bracelet, from Pompeii. L. 9⅜ in.

B. No. 2823. Bracelet, inlaid with glass, provenance unknown. L. 6 in.

C. 1924. 5–14. 12. Necklace, with emerald beads, from Beaurains in France L. 15½ in.

D. 1946. 7–2. 2. Bracelet, provenance unknown. Diam. 3¼ in.

INTRODUCTION

THE British Museum is particularly rich in jewellery of the Greek and Roman world from the earliest times to the death of Constantine, the event which is generally taken to mark the end of the ancient world. The principal material throughout this long period was gold, for which preference there are several reasons. First, rarity; gold has always bestowed a certain cachet on its possessor. Second, beauty; however treated, gold has a colour and a lustre unattainable in any other material. Third, the comparative ease with which it is obtained and worked. Fourth, permanence; the resistance of gold to decay must from earliest times have given to gold a supernatural quality. And finally, convertibility; if hard times come, the possessor of gold can always have recourse to the melting-pot. With gold we include electrum, a natural alloy of gold and silver, which was regarded by the ancients as a white variety of gold.

Silver was also used, chiefly by those who could not afford gold. Base metals, glass, and other substances were also used on occasion for cheaper forms of jewellery, but will not be considered here.

In antiquity, as today, jewellery was predominantly (but not exclusively) a feminine prerogative. Consequently, most of the objects to be discussed were made for female adornment.

9

I. MATERIALS AND METHODS

SHEET METAL is the foundation of most gold jewellery. It is shaped and decorated by means of punches (repoussé work), or with the aid of moulds or stamps.

WIRE is another essential for certain simple basic forms, for the making of ornamental chains, and as a means of decoration, a function which will be discussed below. Throughout most of antiquity it was made from thin strips of sheet metal, which were hammered and rolled until they were round in section. The use of a drawplate (a sheet of metal perforated with holes through which strips of gold are drawn) was not introduced till the end of the Roman period, if as early.

A third, and less important element is CAST METAL. Cast gold jewellery is rare, for it is generally uneconomic, but small objects such as finger-rings, pins, and ear-ring pendants were often so made. The casting was done either directly in stone moulds or indirectly by the lost wax method.

Of the decorative processes, FILIGREE and GRANULATION are the most typical of ancient jewellery. Filigree, the earlier form, consists of wires soldered in patterns on a background. Granulation is a refinement of this technique in which minute grains of gold are substituted for the wire. Filigree never really lost its popularity, but granulation declined in importance in Roman times and finally died out about A.D. 1000. Subsequent attempts to revive it failed until the secret of attaching the grains, for which ordinary soldering methods are too coarse, was rediscovered shortly before the last war.

Another popular method of decoration was INLAYING with coloured stones, glass, or other substances. The inlays are cut to shape and cemented in cells formed by metal strips soldered to the background. A related process, probably derived from the inlaying of glass, is ENAMELLING, which differs from inlay in that the glass is actually fused to the gold background. Powdered glass is placed in the areas to be decorated and the work is fired. When the glass melts it penetrates the metal, which has been softened by the heat. Enamelling is the only goldsmith's process in which the Middle Ages could improve on the work of the ancient craftsmen, for the quality and scope of ancient enamelling is mediocre compared with the work of the Byzantine masters. NIELLO is a process related to enamel, in which a matt black substance, a sulphide of silver, is set in recesses cut in the metal. So far as jewellery is concerned, it is not found before the Roman period.

ENGRAVING was occasionally used for decoration and for the cutting of seals. The chisel was also employed from time to time in carving or in piercing the gold. An example of the latter process is the pierced work of the Romans known as *opus interrasile*.

JOINING was done generally by the same method as was used in connection with filigree and granulation (colloid hard-soldering). A copper salt (probably verdigris) is mixed with glue. Both surfaces are coated with this mixture and brought into contact, so that they adhere. The work is then fired. The copper salt turns to copper oxide, and the glue to carbon. The carbon and oxygen go off as carbon dioxide, leaving a microscopic layer of pure copper between the elements to be joined, and the join is made.

II. GREECE
THE BRONZE AGE
3000–1100 B.C.

THE origins of ancient jewellery lie to the east of the Aegean world, in Babylonia (the modern Iraq) where the cemeteries of the famous city of Ur have yielded magnificent examples of about 2700 B.C. Some of these may be seen in the Department of Western Asiatic Antiquities. The craft spread gradually westward and seems to have reached the Aegean about 2400 B.C., for in cemeteries of this date on the island of Crete we find somewhat unskilled imitations of Babylonian jewellery. None of these objects is represented in the British Museum.

The earliest jewellery here from the Aegean area comprises the so-called Aegina Treasure, a large collection of personal jewellery and gold plate acquired in 1892. The Treasure was stated to have been discovered in a Mycenaean tomb on the island of Aegina, but a recent stylistic examination has shown that this provenance is almost certainly false, since its affinities are almost entirely with Minoan jewellery of the seventeenth and sixteenth centuries B.C.[1] It was in fact probably found in Crete, possibly at Mallia, shortly before reaching the Museum. If this supposition is correct, the Treasure is contemporary with one of the most brilliant periods of the Minoan civilization.

One of the finest pieces is an embossed pendant (pl. 1B), of the seventeenth century B.C., which may have been attached to the head of a dress-pin. A nature-god is represented, standing on a field with lotuses, and holding in either hand a water bird. Although the influence of Egyptian art is strong, he wears the typical Minoan

[1] Minoan is the technical term for the Bronze Age civilization of Crete. It is taken from Minos, the legendary king of Knossos.

costume of drawers, apron, and tight belt. By virtue, no doubt, of his divinity, he also wears an elaborate head-dress and ear-rings. The objects in the background probably represent bows; the circular pendants are perhaps sun-symbols.

Another ornament from this Treasure (pl. 1A), of the same date, comprises a curved plate of gold, terminating at either end in a human head and also hung with circular pendants. The eyes were originally inlaid with coloured stone. This was evidently worn round the neck suspended by a cord or a chain.

Among the five finger-rings in the Treasure, the finest (pl. 2c) has a shield-shaped bezel inlaid with lapis lazuli. This ring is an elaboration of the typical Minoan-Mycenaean ring of pl. 2A, with a long, oval bezel set at right angles to the hoop, a variety with a remarkably long life, ranging from 1800 to 1100 B.C.

Another Minoan ornament, but not from the Aegina Treasure, is a small embossed figure of a goddess (pl. 2D) wearing the character-istic low-cut flounced dress. The origin of this piece, which was probably a dress-ornament, is not known, but it can be dated to the sixteenth century B.C. from the presence of a similar one in one of the Shaft Graves at Mycenae.

This figure serves to introduce the jewellery of the Mycenaean world. The Mycenaean culture, which takes its name from the key-site of Mycenae, was a mainland Greek offshoot of the Minoan. During the sixteenth and fifteenth centuries the two cultures co-existed; in the fourteenth and thirteenth Minoan supremacy was succeeded by that of Mycenae and other Mainland cities. Mycenaean jewellery was deeply indebted to Minoan. The principal differences in the Mycenaean products of this later period are their greater quantity but less adventurous quality. Rightly did Homer call Mycenae 'rich in gold', but her goldsmiths, although initially Mi-noan trained, lacked the inspiration of their masters.

The best of Mycenaean jewellery is in the National Museum in Athens. In London we have isolated pieces from a few mainland sites and from Rhodes. From Cyprus, however, we have a magnifi-cent collection of jewellery, part Mycenaean, part oriental, chiefly from the British Museum excavations at Enkomi of 1896.

EAR-RINGS were not popular on the Greek mainland, but were abundant in Cyprus. Among the commonest types are a tapered hoop (pl. 2K); a hoop composed of a twisted strip of gold (pl. 2J);

and a hoop with a conical, richly granulated pendant (pl. 2 H). They belong to the fourteenth and thirteenth centuries B.C.

On pl. 2 B is a pendant from Cyprus, but of pure Mycenaean form, representing a pomegranate. It was made about 1400 B.C. and, with its superb granulation, is a masterpiece by any standards. Although the art of granulation was introduced into the Aegean area (probably from Syria) as early as about 2000 B.C., it was extremely rare till the fifteenth century B.C., and this pomegranate is the earliest example of it in the British Museum collections.

The typical Mycenaean ornaments are the so-called RELIEF-BEADS, which were strung together and worn as necklaces or round the wrists. They are for the most part pictorial but highly stylized representations of marine or vegetable life, whose artistic origins lie in the Palace Style devised by the vase-painters of Knossos in the later fifteenth century B.C. The best, not represented here, have elaborate granulation and occasionally also enamel. They were mass-produced with stamps and were sometimes strung with beads of the same kind but made of blue glass, imitating lapis lazuli.

On pl. 2 G is a lily bead, probably from Athens; on pl. 2 F a duplicated argonaut-pattern, from Ialysus in Rhodes; on pl. 2 I a stylized shell (or perhaps a flower); and on pl. 2 E a rosette, also from Ialysus.

The typical Mycenaean FINGER-RING is represented in its simplest form by the example on pl. 2 A, from a tomb at Ialysus of the fourteenth century B.C. This type of ring, with a long oval bezel at right angles to the hoop, was taken over from the Minoan repertoire. In the more elaborate examples the bezel is inlaid with coloured stone or glass or is decorated with filigree and granulations. Other varieties were engraved as seals with figured scenes, sometimes of great elaboration.

III. GREECE
DARK AGES AND REVIVAL
1100–600 B.C.

THE Mycenaean world finally collapsed about 1100 B.C., to be succeeded by three centuries of extreme poverty, the so-called Dark Ages. During this period artistic creation was at a low ebb, and articles of jewellery were rare indeed. Soon after 800 B.C., however, contacts with the more civilized East and with Egypt were resumed on a large scale. The jewellery in this age of Greek revival, commonly known as the Orientalizing Period, which covered the eighth and seventh centuries B.C., was again plentiful and of the highest quality. Our source in the British Museum for the Dark Ages and for the eighth century is a collection formed, probably from excavations in Athens, by the seventh Earl of Elgin in the early 1800's.

The Dark Age jewellery was not only rare but primitive, comprising wire spirals to be worn in the hair (pl. 3C shows an example of the eleventh century); ear-rings and bracelets of wire; finger-rings composed of thin strips of gold (pl. 3B and D), and plain diadems of thin sheet gold. In an age of such extreme poverty it is surprising that any gold at all was available; what little they had was probably obtained by looting Mycenaean tombs.

The eighth century saw the production of superb goldwork at certain important centres such as Knossos in Crete, Corinth, and Athens. It is highly probable that immigrant goldsmiths from Phoenicia, which was famed at this date for its craftsmen, settled at these places, set up workshops, and taught the secrets of their trade to local apprentices. Much of the jewellery of the eighth century rather puzzlingly recalls that of the Mycenaean period, some five centuries earlier. We know that there can have been no continuity of tradition in Greek lands, and the only possible explanation is that

16

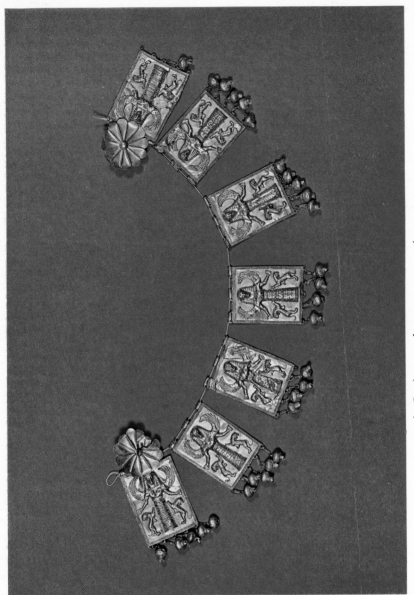

A. Greek pectoral ornaments, seventh century B.C.

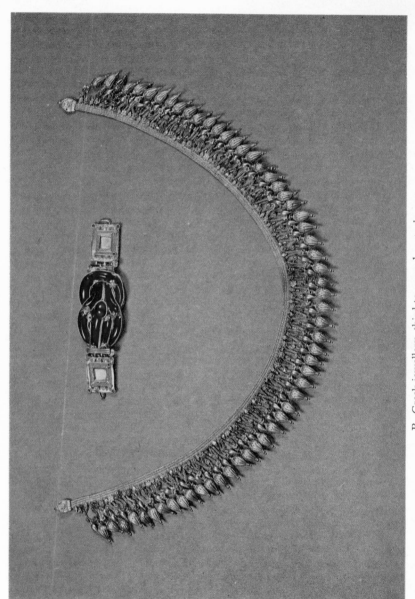

B. Greek jewellery, third to second centuries B.C.

Mycenaean fashions found their way to the coasts of the Levant, where they were kept alive by the Phoenicians throughout the Dark Ages and reintroduced to the Greek world when it was once more in a position to enjoy the luxuries of life.

On pl. 3F is a crescent-shaped ear-ring decorated with granulation of a higher quality even than the best Mycenaean work. The enclosed areas held inlay, probably of crystal or amber, which has now perished. It is hung with cord-like chains carrying simple finials. Pl. 3E shows another Athenian ear-ring of the eighth century B.C., a disk equipped with a bulbous 'tail'. Disk and tail have granulation finer even than that of the other ear-ring, and were also originally inlaid. The earring was worn suspended from a hook inserted in the lobe of the ear.

A dress-accessory which seldom aspired to the status of jewellery is the FIBULA or safety-pin, a useful article when clothing was draped rather than tailored to the body. A common eighth-century type had a large square plate attached to the safety-catch, which served as a ground for engraved designs. Few such fibulae have survived in gold, but the Elgin collection boasts four, making up two pairs. One example (pl. 3A) has an engraving on one side of the catch-plate of a grazing deer; on the other side a swastika. Other subjects on other fibulae are a horse, a lion, and a ship.

In the seventh century the best jewellery comes no longer from Athens but from the Islands and Asia Minor. The principal sources for the British Museum are the cemeteries of Camirus in Rhodes, excavated in the 1860's, and the Temple of Artemis at Ephesus, excavated in 1904–5.

A Rhodian diadem is shown on pl. 4 F, composed of a strip of gold with rosettes made separately and attached. The characteristic Rhodian ornament of this date is a set of decorated rectangular plaques worn across the breast and secured at the ends by pins (Colour pl. A). These pectoral ornaments were embossed by means of stamps and the best of them were also skilfully granulated. It has been estimated that a plaque like that on pl. 4 E contains not less than 2,600 grains. The plaque illustrated has a sphinx, with three human heads below. The strongly Egyptianizing faces are typical of seventh-century Greek art; the style is known as Dedalic, after Daedalus, the mythical craftsman. Other subjects include a winged goddess with lions, an Asiatic deity associated by the Greeks with

Artemis (Colour pl. A); the so-called 'Astarte at the Window'; a centaur; and a bee-goddess.

Closely related to the Rhodian tradition is an exquisite class of rosettes made for attachment to diadems of cloth or leather but of the general form of pl. 4 F. Most surviving examples have been found on the island of Melos, and that is doubtless where they were made (pl. 4 D). They are decorated with human and animal heads, insects, and flowers.

We come now to the jewellery from Ephesus. This was excavated on the site of the Temple of Artemis (the Roman Diana)—not that visited by St. Paul but its predecessor. It was deposited as a votive offering to the Goddess, but was made to be worn. This jewellery falls almost entirely within the seventh century. The style has much in common with the Island jewellery, but, as might be expected, the oriental element is stronger. A selection on pl. 4 A–C shows a circular brooch, a drum-headed dress-pin, and another brooch in the form of a hawk.

IV. GREECE
ARCHAIC AND CLASSICAL PERIODS
600–330 B.C.

AFTER about 600 B.C. jewellery became extremely scarce in Greek lands, and remained so for some 150 years. We can only surmise that supplies of gold were cut off by the Persians, who were in the ascendancy in the Middle East over most of this period. Continuity was, however, assured, for at this time we find evidence of Greek goldsmiths working for foreign patrons abroad.

When the curtain lifts again after the final defeat of the Persians, about 450 B.C., we find jewellery made in the same unbroken tradition, but with certain significant changes. Filigree has replaced the more laborious process of granulation, and enamel (not seen since Mycenaean times) has been reintroduced, and in a more sophisticated form. It was now used in conjunction with filigree, but always sparingly, so as to let the beauty of the gold speak for itself.

During the so-called Classical period between the Persian defeat[1] and the conquests of Alexander in the later fourth century B.C., some of the finest works of art of all time were produced, and the best of the goldwork is fit to rank with these masterpieces.

WREATHS, whether of natural leaves or imitations of nature in precious metals, were worn in the Classical period at parties and in processions and were buried with the dead. Few surviving examples in precious metals are stout enough to have been worn by the living, but one of silver on pl. 5 is an exception. It is a close imitation of myrtle, a variety especially popular for wreaths: in its natural state it was sacred to Aphrodite, and it had the additional advantage at parties of dispelling the fumes of wine.

EAR-RINGS took several forms. One of the basic shapes with a

---

[1] We generally start the Classical period about 480 B.C., but for jewellery 450 is a more suitable date.

very long history is the spiral. A late-fifth-century example is strikingly decorated with pyramids and lozenges of granulation (pl. 6 A). Another kind of spiral was common in Cyprus in the fifth century. It terminates in a griffin's head of truly fearsome aspect, the transition between spiral and head being masked by a collar of blue and green enamel (pl. 6 B).

A second type of ear-ring is a disk which was worn in a slit in the ear-lobe. Many such ear-studs, as we should properly call them, have been found in Rhodes: one, of the fifth century, is embossed with a scene of the sea-nymph Thetis riding a dolphin and carrying a helmet to Achilles her son (pl. 6 G).

Boat-shaped ear-rings were also popular. An unusually elaborate example of the late fifth century (one of a pair) is shown on pl. 6 D. From a large enamelled rosette hangs the basic boat-shape, decorated with filigree and enamel; from this hang cockle-shell pendants on chains, and on it sits a minute figure of a siren (a human-headed bird). Such complexity might well lead to confusion, but it is in fact triumphantly successful.

From their decoration, four recently acquired rosettes are shown to be contemporary with these ear-rings; one is illustrated on pl. 6 F. They are composed of a double sheet of gold cut into eight petals. In the centre is a smaller rosette, enamelled in white and green, from which radiate out lifelike stamens. The purpose of these rosettes, which are equipped with a stout 'stalk' behind, is a mystery, but they evidently represent some member of the buttercup family.

Gold FINGER-RINGS are fairly common in this period. The bezels, either circular (pl. 6 E) or pointed-oval (pl. 6 C), were sometimes engraved as seals, sometimes embossed with designs in relief.

NECKLACES are not common, but the few surviving examples are of very high quality. One of the finest, on pl. 7, comes from Tarentum, a prosperous Greek settlement on the site of the modern Taranto, where it was made in the early fourth century. The necklace is composed of interlocking rosettes and other ornaments, from which hang buds and human heads. The play of light and shade on the surface of the gold is extraordinarily effective.

The usual form of BRACELET at this date is a rod or tube bent almost into a circle and equipped at either end with animal-head finials. That on pl. 8 A with ram's heads comes from a tomb in Cyprus of the fifth century. An unusual variation, with pony's heads, is shown on pl. 8 B. The hoop is good Greek work of the fourth century, but the heads, their eyes and ears inlaid with blue glass, are purely Scythian in appearance. The bracelet must have been made for a Scythian customer by a Greek goldsmith of one of the Black Sea settlements.

V. GREECE
THE HELLENISTIC PERIOD
330–27 B.C.

THIS chapter is concerned with the so-called Hellenistic period, which was initiated by the conquests of Alexander the Great between 333 and 322 B.C. and came to an end with the inauguration of the Roman Empire in 27 B.C. Alexander's conquests altered every aspect of Greek life, and jewellery was no exception. In the first place, Hellenistic jewellery is remarkably plentiful, for the exploitation of the Macedonian mines and the dissipation of the captured Persian treasures made gold more accessible to the Greeks than ever before.

In the second place, close contacts with Egypt and Western Asia created a taste for enriching goldwork with coloured stones and glass to an extent which had not been seen since Mycenaean times. A wide variety of stones was employed: cornelian, chalcedony, amethyst, occasionally small pearls, but above all, garnets. The Hellenistic jewellers discovered, as the Victorians were to rediscover, the mutual enhancement of gold and garnet.

In the third place, new types of ornament and new motifs were introduced from the newly conquered territories. These innovations were not immediate in their effect, but succeeded gradually in transforming the somewhat austere fashions of the Classical era. The most important centres of jewellery production in the Hellenistic world were probably the cities of Alexandria and Antioch.

The terracotta figure on pl. 9 will serve to illustrate the jewellery of a Hellenistic lady of the second century B.C. The original of the portrait was, it must be admitted, Etruscan and not truly Greek, but Etruscan jewellery at this date was for all practical purposes Greek, and she may legitimately be used as evidence for Greek fashions. She wears a pointed diadem, ear-rings with pendants of red stones, a strap-necklace with pendants, circular brooches on her shoulders, and also (not included in the photograph) bracelets and finger-rings. This equipment can be paralleled very closely from jewellery in the Museum.

The most elaborate type of DIADEM of the third and second centuries B.C. is unfortunately represented in the Museum only by a fragment. In the centre of these diadems is a richly decorated Heracles knot (a reef-knot, which was credited with magical powers), often inlaid with garnets and decorated in other ways. The central portion of such a diadem, illustrated on Colour pl. B, is one of the finest surviving. The knot is completely inlaid with superb garnets and decorated with small rosettes enamelled in dark blue and green. The plates at either side are enamelled in the same colours. The missing diadem would have consisted of a strap or a frame of gold, hung with pendants of great complexity. Those masterpieces of Hellenistic jewellery were only for the millionaire class, and were virtually restricted to the rich communities of South Russia and the Macedonian kingdom.

Pl. 11 A shows a simpler DIADEM not far removed from that on pl. 9. Found in a tomb of the early third century B.C., it is decorated pictorially with a combination of low relief and filigree.

Hellenistic EAR-RINGS are extremely plentiful. A new variety, which rapidly attained popularity, is a hoop of coiled wire tapering to a point at one end and equipped at the other with a human, or more commonly an animal's head: favourite subjects are lions, horned lions (a monster of Persian origin), bulls, goats, or gazelles. One of the last kind, with inlaid eyes and brow of garnet, is shown on pl. 10 B. Towards the end of the Hellenistic period the type was enlivened by threading the hoop with coloured stones or glass. Dolphin's heads are particularly common with this decoration (pl. 10 A).

The ear-ring on pl. 10 E is of the kind worn by the lady on pl. 9, and is another popular variety. From a gold disk hangs a pendant in the form of a gold-framed garnet. Other equally popular pendants include figures of Eros (a naked winged boy: pl. 10 D), Victory (a winged woman), a bird, or a jar.

FINGER-RINGS of the Classical type continued well into the Hellenistic period, but new styles were also developed. Of these one of the finest has a bezel composed of a large *cabochon*-cut stone, garnet, or amethyst (pl. 10 G). Another attractive variety is made to resemble a coiled snake (pl. 10 F).

A brooch with an embossed design (pl. 10 C) serves to explain the circular object on the lady's shoulder on pl. 9. Brooches of this kind now began to replace the long pins used in the Classical period for fastening the dress on the shoulders.

Hellenistic NECKLACES are not perhaps as fine as the best of the fifth and fourth century, but they are much more numerous, and were evidently within the reach of a larger section of the population. Colour pl. B shows the kind worn by the lady of pl. 9. The basis is a strap-like object which looks at first sight to be plaited, but which is in fact composed of links of very fine chain interlinked side by side. The straps are hung, either directly or from chains, with small pendants in the form of spear-heads or (as here) jars. Joins in the chains are marked by tiny enamelled ornaments. Temple treasure-records from the island of Delos list just such necklaces among the offerings to Artemis of the early third century B.C.

Another popular necklace, especially towards the end of this period, consists of linked beads, often gold-capped garnets, with animal-head finials like those on contemporary hoop ear-rings. Indeed, matching sets of necklace and ear-rings were very popular amongst well-to-do Hellenistic ladies. On pl. 11B is a necklace of this kind, terminating in the heads of wild goats.

BRACELETS became increasingly popular. On pl. 11C is a late-fourth-century development of the type shown on pl. 8 A. The hoop is slimmer, like that of the Graeco-Scythian bracelet on pl. 8 B, and the bull's head finials are paralleled on contemporary ear-rings. The junction between the hoop and the heads is masked by a collar of garnet. This bracelet, with its fellow, comes from a large collection of jewellery found at Cyme in Asia Minor and belonging to the late fourth or early third century B.C.

VI. ETRURIA

700–250 B.C.

ALTHOUGH we are familiar with the culture of the Etruscan people, their origins are still a mystery. It seems, however, that the earliest Etruscans migrated to Italy from Asia Minor in the late eighth century B.C. and settled in that part of central Italy which is still known after them as Tuscany. The period of the greatest power, and their finest jewellery, covers the seventh and sixth centuries B.C. Politically the decline began shortly after the beginning of the fifth century B.C., and continued till the middle of the third century, when the Etruscan cities were finally defeated and absorbed by the growing power of Rome. But for reasons which are not clear, there was something of a renaissance in Etruscan art about 400 B.C., which continued for some 150 years.

Etruscan jewellery is best considered in two phases: Early Etruscan, of the seventh to fifth centuries B.C., and Late Etruscan, 400 to 250 B.C. After 250 B.C. there was still plenty of jewellery being made in Etruria, but it was now purely Hellenistic in style, a fact which explains how an Etruscan portrait-figure of the second century B.C. could be admitted as evidence for Hellenistic jewellery (see p. 22).

Early Etruscan jewellery is characterized by its abundance, its technical perfection, and its variety. The technical knowledge must have reached the Etruscans from the same Phoenician sources as supplied the Greeks in the eighth century, but the Etruscans made different use of it. Granulation was the decorative process *par excellence*. The work is as fine as the best Greek work, and in addition the Etruscans developed the possibilities of this technique to a far higher degree than did the Greeks. Not only were the grains disposed in simple patterns, but whole scenes were portrayed in silhouettes of granulation, or, by a reversed process, the figures were in relief and the background granulated; or the whole surface was covered with gold dust.

Filigree was at first used sparingly, but on occasion was applied in open-work patterns without a background, an extremely difficult process which was never attempted in Greece.

Towards the end of the seventh century, Greek influence first made itself felt, not so much in the forms of the jewellery as in new decorative motifs and technical innovations, such as an increased use of filigree and the introduction of inlay and enamelling. These changes should probably be explained by the arrival of immigrant Greek goldsmiths, whose lack of work at home in the sixth century is mentioned above (p. 19).

Among the finest examples of seventh-century Etruscan jewellery are BRACELETS of great elaboration. On pl. 12 A is a strip of gold (one of a pair) decorated with intricate patterns in the finest granulation, and with attached human figures. Pl. 12 B shows another bracelet, also one of a pair, this one with figures of embossed and granulated work.

FIBULAE played a much greater part in Etruscan jewellery than in Greek. A number of different varieties were in use in the seventh century, all probably inherited from the precursors of the Etruscans in central Italy. One of the finest, from Vulci, is shown on Colour pl. C. The basic form of the fibula is almost completely encrusted with figures in the round, sphinxes, lions, lion's heads, horse's heads; and everything is richly granulated. The fibula is, to modern taste, smothered by the decoration, but as an example of the virtuosity of the Etruscan goldsmith it is without a rival.

EAR-RINGS were made in several kinds. A seventh-century variety, also from Vulci, is shown on pl. 13 A. It consists of a disk notched at the top, and cut with a chisel into open-work patterns.

The Etruscan ear-ring *par excellence* belongs chiefly to the sixth century (pl. 13 B). It is generally known as the *baule* type, so called by the Italians from its resemblance to a valise, and consists of a strip of gold bent into a cylindrical form and closed by a disk at either end. The hook for insertion in the ear is masked, in the example illustrated, by a semicircular strip. The ear-ring is richly decorated with filigree and occasional touches of enamel, and above all with figures of berries, flowers, and the like, made separately and attached in small panels. These ear-rings are among the finest of Etruscan inventions.

Another sixth-century ear-ring of less originality is a disk. The example on pl. 13C is opulently decorated with granulation, filigree, applied ornament, and glass inlay. These disks sometimes reach an astonishing size, but there is good evidence of their purpose in contemporary terracotta figures.

The early Etruscans loved colour and their necklaces of delicately granulated gold beads frequently included also glass and faience beads of Phoenician origin. That illustrated on pl. 13 D is a striking example, of the seventh century, of the effectiveness of this polychrome style.

Late Etruscan jewellery, of about 400 to 250 B.C., is completely different in form and in execution, consisting as it does of large convex surfaces of sheet gold. Decoration is meagre: filigree and granulation were occasionally used, but in general the goldsmith restricted himself to embossed patterns of the simplest kind. The repertoire was as limited as the style: flimsy wreaths for burial with the dead, ear-rings, necklaces, bracelets, and finger-rings. After the elaboration of the earlier jewellery we might expect to find such simplicity a refreshing change, but it is not so, and it is no wonder that Hellenistic fashions were adopted so avidly when they became familiar in the course of the third century B.C.

On pl. 14 A and 14 C are typical Late Etruscan EAR-RINGS: large and showy, but lacking in inspiration. The FINGER-RING on pl. 14 B has more to recommend it. So has the NECKLACE on pl. 14 D, whose large pendant-beads are not unattractive; the circular variety is the BULLA, an amulet worn by Etruscans. Its use was passed on to the Romans, who knew it as the *Etruscum aurum*, the Etruscan gold ornament *par excellence*.

VII. THE ROMAN EMPIRE

27 B.C.–A.D. 337

THIS chapter will deal with the jewellery of the Roman Empire from its inauguration in 27 B.C. down to the death of Constantine the Great in A.D. 337. But first, a word about republican and pre-republican Rome. For long jewellery was one of those luxuries under official disapproval, and surviving examples are not only very scarce, but purely derivative in style. We may indeed equate early Roman jewellery with Etruscan, and classify it accordingly as Early Etruscan, down to 400 B.C.; Late Etruscan, 400–250 B.C.; and Hellenistic, 250–27 B.C.

At the time when this chapter begins Rome had annexed virtually all the Hellenistic world, and the old ideals of austerity were quickly forgotten. In artistic matters Rome, as we know, was always deeply in the debt of Greece, and the jewellery of the early Empire was, in many respects, simply a continuation of Hellenistic. During the three and a half centuries under review, however, certain other influences were felt, and by the end of this period much Roman jewellery was leading the way to the Byzantine style which was to follow.

In brief, jewellery at the beginning of this period was essentially a development of Late Hellenistic, except that certain articles (e.g. pl. 15 A) seem to perpetuate the Late Etruscan love of unbroken rounded surfaces. It was essentially a gold jewellery. Towards the end of the period, however, an increasing emphasis was placed on stones for their own sake, and less pains were taken over the working of the gold in which they were set. Here for the first time the very hardest stones were used: diamonds occasionally, although they were not cut; sapphires, and above all, emeralds, from the newly

28

discovered Egyptian mines in the Red Sea hills, which were used in the natural hexagonal prisms in which these stones are found.

One form of goldworking was, however, popular towards the end of this period, and that is a kind of metal-fretwork, called by the Romans *opus interrasile*, in which patterns are cut out of sheet gold with a chisel. This process was further developed in Byzantine jewellery.

Inlaying was still practised. Enamel was seldom used, but a related form of decoration, NIELLO, made its first appearance in ancient jewellery.

The chief centres of production were probably, as before, Alexandria and Antioch, and now also Rome itself, whither many immigrant craftsmen from the Greek East had migrated. We have evidence that goldsmiths and silversmiths were now organized in guilds like medieval craftsmen.

As an example of the love of finery under the early Empire, especially among the *nouveaux-riches*, we may recall a passage in the *Satyricon* of Petronius, in which Trimalchio calls for scales in the middle of dinner to weigh the combined jewellery worn by himself and his wife.

The destruction of Pompeii and Herculaneum in A.D. 79 is a useful dating point for the early part of this period; some jewellery from Pompeii is exhibited. For the later part of the period we have various deposits, funerary and otherwise, dated by coins.

EAR-RINGS take several forms. Hoops of various kinds continued from the Hellenistic period, but more characteristically Roman is the ball ear-ring, which was found in great numbers at Pompeii (pl. 15 A). These ear-rings, which are composed basically of a hemisphere of gold, recall the spirit of Late Etruscan jewellery, but in the present state of our knowledge no such connexion can be traced through the intervening Hellenistic period. Sometimes the gold surface is replaced by clusters of tiny emeralds (pl. 15 c) or seed-pearls.

Another type, which was destined to become popular in the Byzantine period, comprises a horizontal bar hanging from a mounted stone; from the bar hang two or three drop-pendants. A fine example of the third century A.D., inlaid with magnificent garnets, is shown on pl. 15 B.

NECKLACES with linked stones in gold settings were taken over direct from the Hellenistic repertoire. On Colour pl. D is shown an attractive necklace in this style, of the first century A.D. It is formed of chains and mounted stones. More mounted stones are attached to make a butterfly-shaped pendant. Sapphires, garnets, and crystals are combined with telling effect.

Another type of necklace was a Roman invention of the latter part of this period. Beads in the form of the natural hexagonal crystals of emerald are threaded on a chain. The example illustrated on pl. 16 c comes from a deposit at Beaurains near Arras dated by coins about A.D. 300.

Three BRACELETS of the first century A.D. are illustrated. One, from Pompeii, made of linked gold balls in the style of the ball-ear-rings, is shown on pl. 16 A. Another variety, represented at Pompeii, takes the form of a remarkably lifelike snake, probably a cobra (pl. 16 D). Finally, an unusually handsome bracelet (pl. 16 B). It has a centre-piece in the form of a large vase, with wings below the handles; on it and round it are inlaid squares of green glass imitating emeralds. An ornamental band of gold formed the bracelet itself; in the illustration it is shown spread out to the left of the centre-piece. It is decorated with a plaited band and with open-work leaves and berries.

FINGER-RINGS were extremely popular under the Empire. Under the Republic, the wearing of a gold ring was a privilege awarded to few, but under the early Empire it was bestowed more and more freely, and was soon open to all. Rings were worn by the Romans as marks of dignity, as seals, and as tokens of betrothal (but not of marriage). The wearing of rings by both sexes became so popular that the satirist Martial (who should not be taken too seriously) complains of a man who wore six rings on every finger.

On pl. 15G is a gold ring from Beaurains of about A.D. 300 with a bezel of beryl and an inscription in niello PATERNA and VALE-RIANUS: probably a betrothal ring. On pl. 15 F is a fourth-century ring with patterns in pierced work (*opus interrasile*). And on pl. 15 E is one set with a magnificent emerald. Gold coins were also set in rings and worn perhaps as a mark of military distinction as medals are worn today.

FIBULAE were used by the Romans, as by the Etruscans, for fastening their dress; the Roman fibula, however, was not derived from the Etruscan, but was reintroduced into Italy by the Celts. The commonest Roman fibula, the so-called crossbow type (pl. 15 D) flourished in the third and fourth centuries A.D.

EPILOGUE

In this booklet we have traced the art of jewellery in Classical lands for some 2,500 years. The development has not been a gradual process, but rather a series of spurts. The impetus for these spurts seems to have come in every instance from the East, and if the study were to be continued into Byzantine times, we would see yet another repetition of the process, for the East is the true home of this art.

Yet what is important in this context is not so much what was borrowed as what was made of the borrowings. Our theme, in fact, is how, with their characteristic genius, the Greeks (and, to a lesser extent, the Etruscans and the Romans) transformed what they took, and at times achieved results beyond the powers of their oriental masters.

BIBLIOGRAPHY

GENERAL WORKS

BECATTI, G. *Oreficerie antiche dalle minoiche alle barbariche* (Rome, 1955).
COCHE DE LA FERTÉ, E. *Les Bijoux antiques* (Paris, 1956).
HIGGINS, R. A. *Greek and Roman Jewellery* (London, 1961).
HOFFMANN, H. and DAVIDSON, P. F. *Greek Gold* (Mainz, 1965).

CATALOGUES AND GUIDES

BRITISH MUSEUM. (1) Marshall, F. H. *Catalogue of the Jewellery . . . in the Departments of Antiquities, British Museum* (1911). (2) Id. *Catalogue of the Finger Rings . . . in the Departments of Antiquities, British Museum* (1907).
ATHENS, NATIONAL MUSEUM. (1) (Stathatos Coll.). Amandry, P. *Collection H. Stathatos*, i (Strasbourg, 1953), iii (Strasbourg, 1963). (2) (Mycenae, Shaft Graves). Karo, G. *Schachtgräber von Mykenai* (Berlin, 1930).
ATHENS, BENAKI MUSEUM. Segall, B. *Museum Benaki. Katalog d. Goldschmiede-Arbeiten* (Athens, 1938).
BERLIN, STAATLICHE MUSEEN. Bruns, G. *Schatzkammer der Antike* (Berlin, 1946).
NAPLES, MUSEO NAZIONALE. (1) Breglia, L. *Le oreficerie del Museo Nazionale di Napoli* (Rome, 1941). (2) Siviero, R. *Gli ori e le ambre nel Museo Nazionale di Napoli* (Florence, 1954).
NEW YORK, METROPOLITAN MUSEUM. Alexander, C. *Jewellery. The Art of the Goldsmith in Classical Times* (New York, 1928).

C. Etruscan fibula, seventh century B.C.

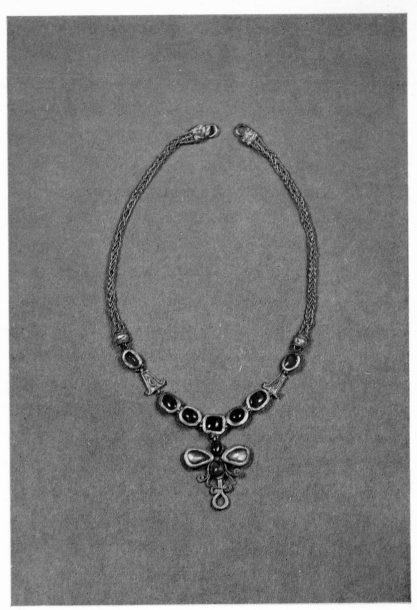

D. Roman necklace, first century A.D.

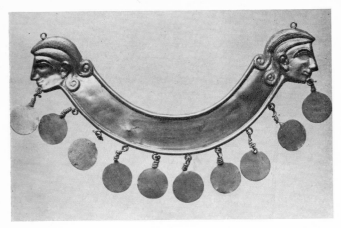

A

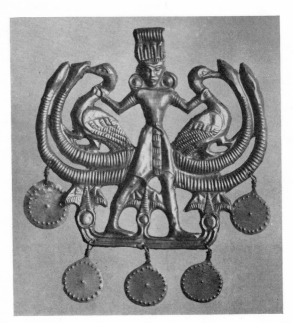

B

1. Minoan jewellery, seventeenth century B.C,

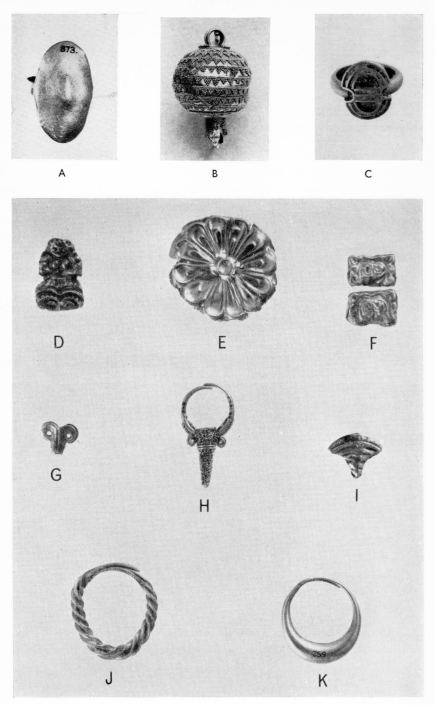

2. Minoan and Mycenaean jewellery, sixteenth to thirteenth centuries B.C.

A

B   C   D

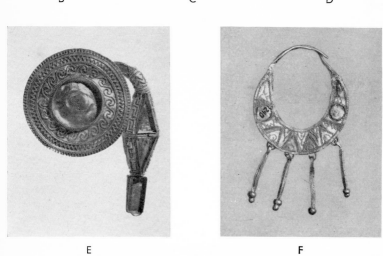

E   F

3. Greek jewellery, eleventh to eighth centuries B.C.

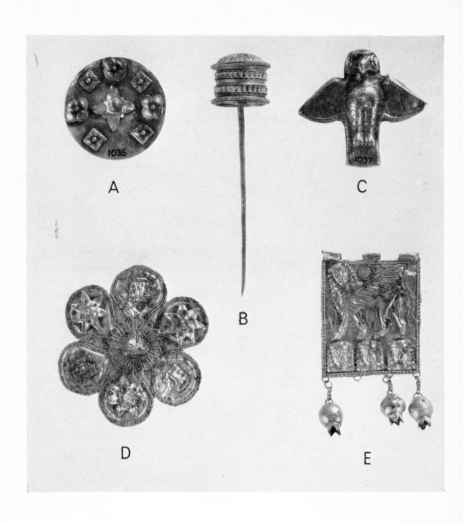

4. Greek jewellery, seventh century B.C.

5. Greek silver wreath, fifth century B.C.

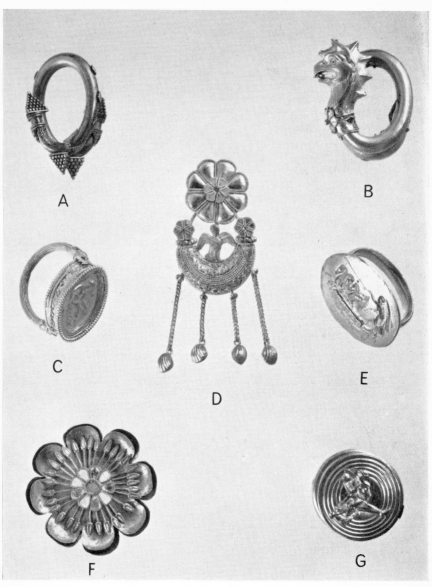

6. Greek jewellery, fifth to fourth centuries B.C.

7. Greek necklace, fourth century B.C.

A

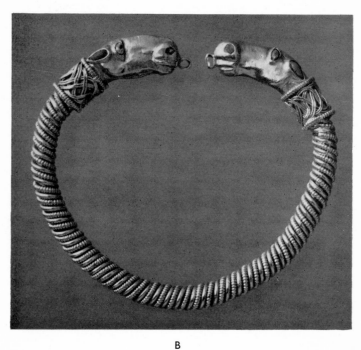

B

8. Greek bracelets, fifth to fourth centuries B.C.

9. Woman wearing Hellenistic jewellery, second century B.C.

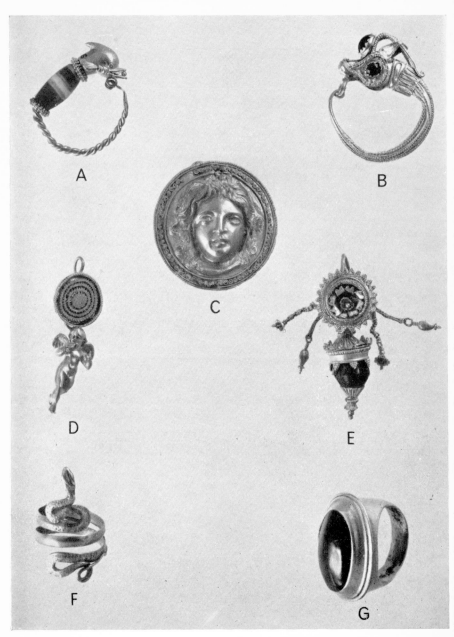

10. Hellenistic jewellery, 330–27 B.C.

A

C

B

11. Hellenistic jewellery, 330–27 B.C.

A   B

12. Etruscan bracelets, seventh century B.C.

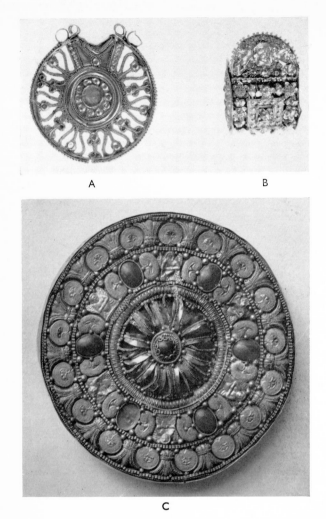

A   B

C

D

13. Etruscan jewellery, seventh to sixth centuries B.C.

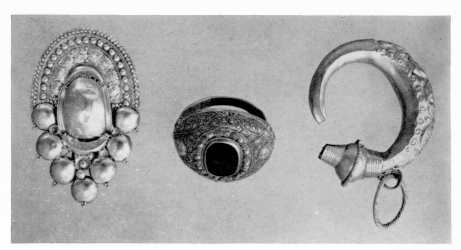

A   B   C

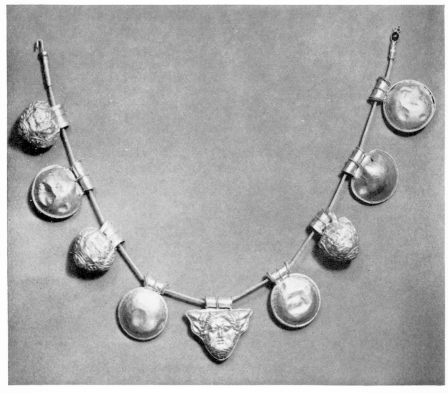

D

14. Etruscan jewellery, 400–250 B.C.

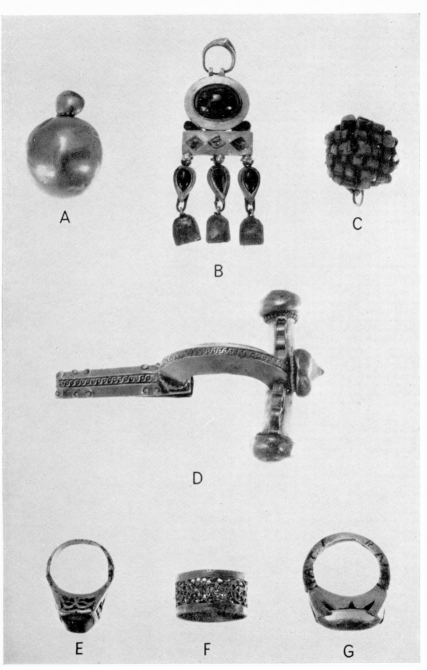

15. Roman jewellery, 27 B.C.–A.D. 337.

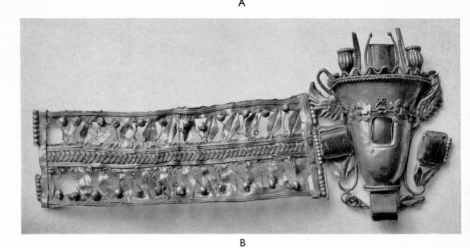

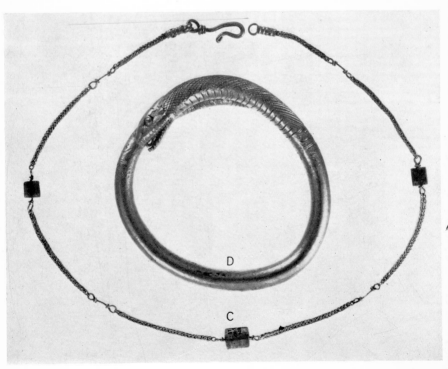

16. Roman jewellery, 27 B.C.–A.D. 337.